ORFORD CASTLE

SUFFOLK

❖

John Rhodes

Throughout his long reign (1154–89) Henry II, though a most formidable ruler, suffered endless adversities – from his rebellious barons, his troublesome family, and his one-time friend, Thomas Becket. Orford Castle was built in response to some of these difficulties.

The castle is of particular interest now for its unique design and as the earliest English castle with surviving building accounts for the whole period of its construction. Henry intended his new castle to proclaim his authority to the barons of East Anglia, especially Hugh Bigod, Earl of Norfolk, and to protect the coast from foreign attack. Designed as a visible symbol of royal superiority as much as a military stronghold, it showed how castles could be grand domestic residences as well as defensive structures. Construction also gave impetus to the development of Orford itself, with a new church, new street plan, and improved port facilities.

As soon as completed, the castle helped to defeat rebellion by the united forces of Henry's queen and sons, the French king and the ageing but implacable Bigod. Orford was to remain an important royal castle for another 150 years, controlled by the king's constable and serving as military stronghold and centre of local administration.

Henry II's keep survives to its full height, still dominating Orford and the length of Suffolk coast where it stands. The panorama from the roof takes in a dramatic sweep of land and sea and the long shingle spit of Orford Ness.

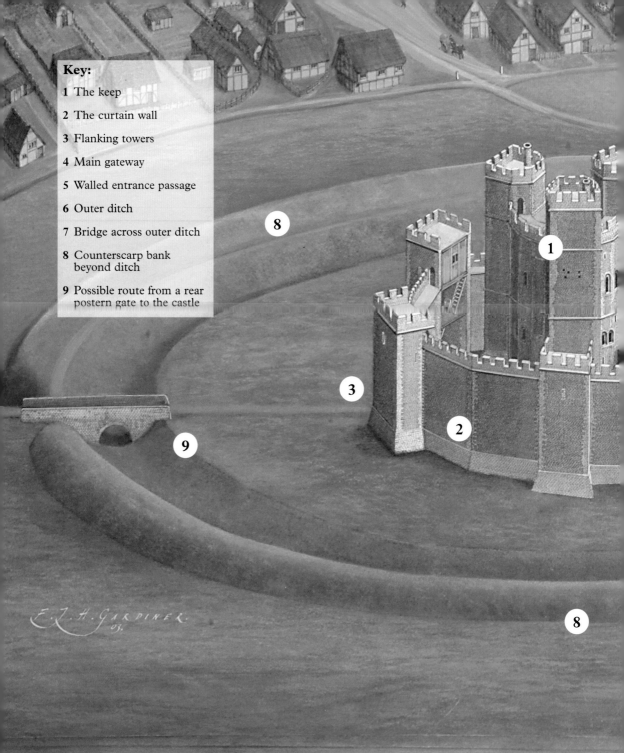

Key:

1 The keep

2 The curtain wall

3 Flanking towers

4 Main gateway

5 Walled entrance passage

6 Outer ditch

7 Bridge across outer ditch

8 Counterscarp bank beyond ditch

9 Possible route from a rear postern gate to the castle

TOUR OF THE CASTLE

❖

Before walking up to the castle from the carpark, it is worth trying to imagine its layout when first built, for one vital element of the original castle has now vanished. The keep survives to its full height of nearly 30 metres, but it once stood within a court or bailey, enclosed by a curtain wall with towers and surrounded by a deep defensive ditch. If these outer defences were captured, the garrison could still hold out in the keep.

The curtain walls were punctuated with towers, which allowed defenders to direct crossbow fire at attackers along the wall's outer face. Virtually all traces of the wall had disappeared by the 1840s and the remaining banks and ditches have been distorted by digging for stone or sand. It is worthwhile, however, to try and keep these lost defences in mind as we explore the castle.

FRANK GARDNER

Reconstruction drawing of Orford Castle looking east towards the town, as it may have appeared about 1300. By this date many of the timber fortifications erected by Henry II, such as the outer palisade, had probably disappeared. The drawing is based on early illustrations of the castle and on surveys and excavations carried out during 2002–3. There is more discussion about the now-vanished walls and towers on pages 8–9 of the guidebook

THE OUTSIDE VIEW

The keep, built between 1165 and 1173, is remarkably well preserved, little altered since it was built. Such great towers were a regular part of 12th-century castles, but Orford's design is unusual – cylindrical inside, polygonal outside, and buttressed by three turrets. Most keeps at the time were rectangular in plan, like that of Henry II's great castle at Dover. The compact design of Orford was highly sophisticated, experimenting with new techniques of defence as well as creating a grand and, by Norman standards, comfortable residence.

The keep contains two circular halls, one above the other, marked on the outside of the central tower by the two levels of window openings. Each hall has its own two-storey suite of rooms, arranged within the turrets and the thickness of the walls. These rooms are lit by smaller slit windows.

Within the sloping plinth is a basement for storage, and from the roof and turrets there are wide views over land and sea.

The nearest turret as you approach the keep contains the main stair, connecting all floors. Inside the building, as you will see, details of ingenious domestic and defensive arrangements make for a rewarding exploration. The whole layout and appearance of the keep reveal the mind of a creative designer, concerned with comfort and convenience and with harmonious external proportions, based on precise geometrical calculations.

Three main types of stone are visible in the building. Sandy oolitic limestone from Northamptonshire was used for the plinth, for the quoins where walls meet at an angle, and for door- and window-openings. Caen stone, from Henry's dukedom of Normandy, was used for finer work, especially inside the building. Both of these arrived at the site by sea. More local were the squared blocks of clayey limestone called septaria, dredged from the coast and estuaries, which make up the main panels of walling. It is soft and weathers badly, and the keep was probably rendered to protect it from the rain and winds off the sea. There is also some use, mostly inside the building, of the local sandy, shell-rich Coralline Crag, dug from the quarry south-west of the castle or from a similar local pit.

Dover Castle, with its great square keep built by Henry II in the 1180s. The keep at Orford was built to a more unusual, experimental design

© SKYSCAN BALLOON PHOTOGRAPHY

NORWICH CASTLE MUSEUM AND ART GALLERY

ENTRANCE TO THE KEEP

The path up to the keep is not the original approach, but cuts across the earthworks and the line of the former curtain wall. The last fragment of wall, to the right of the path, collapsed on 1 July 1841 'with a tremendous crash'. More is said about the vanished defences on pages 8-9. The only access into the tower is through the first-floor doorway of the forebuilding.

Go up the stairs to enter the keep.

Half the height of the main tower, the forebuilding contains the entrance lobby, with a small chapel above. The outer stair is 19th century, but it follows the line of the original; you can trace the curving line of the wall which once protected it. There also seems to have been a porch – note the triangle of dressed stone over the doorway. The door is modern, but the triangular arch above it is medieval, similar to others you will see inside the building.

ENTRANCE LOBBY

This small, dignified space was where important visitors could be received, or lesser folk identified before being allowed further. The way into the Lower Hall, through the 3-metre-thick wall of the main tower, lies

Orford Castle and village, painted by Henry Bright in 1856 from the area of sand quarrying to the west

The entrance doorway and approach stair. The 19th-century stone stair follows the line of the 12th-century original

The triple arches with decorative capitals which frame the triangular-headed entrance doorway to the passage

Lower right: 17th- and 18th-century graffiti, carved on the sides of the passage to the Lower Hall

Plan of Level Two (entrance)

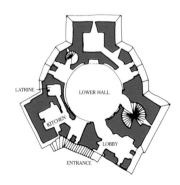

beneath the beautifully formed triple arch, with ornamental carved capitals on its right-hand side and arches fanning out to fit the triangular space available. Within this small area is a group of defensive features designed to protect the Hall. Above the outer doorway are the grooves down which a heavy portcullis descended to bar the entrance, while the two doorways in the passage to the Hall have slots in the walls each side from which massive beams could be drawn to bolt the doors firmly shut. As you explore the castle, look out for other devices for bolting or barring the doors.

Above the passage doorways, on the Hall side, notice also the heavy protruding stone blocks, designed to prevent the doors being lifted from their hinges by an attacking force. Beneath the lobby, entered by means of a trapdoor in the floor, is a small

basement room not accessible to visitors. It has its own latrine and may have been used by the porter on entrance duty, but it seems more likely to have been built as a prison chamber. This is by no means always the case with dark rooms in castle basements, but at Orford there are records of a succession of medieval prisoners (including Orford's Merman – see page 28), and this is probably the place where, with maximum security, they were held captive.

LOWER HALL

Walk into the main hall.

The castle was a defended residence, although for much of the time it was virtually empty, administered by the king's constable with maybe a few servants, a porter, and a small garrison. But it had occasionally to take in large gatherings of people – when it was fully garrisoned during a crisis (there were perhaps twenty knights and a larger number of men-at-arms at Orford in 1174) or when a noble or royal household visited. The retinue of officials, servants and men-at-arms, with their horses and baggage, would then have filled the castle with noise and activity. The keep also had to accommodate sessions of the manorial or criminal courts, since the castle, under the constable, was a local centre of administration and justice, where disputes were settled and judgements delivered.

The Lower Hall was the more public space for such gatherings, in contrast with the grander but more private Upper Hall. The stone bench round the wall provided seating for an assembly, a court session, or a feast. Some might have to sleep here afterwards; there were never enough bed spaces for everyone, though further room was available in the buildings of the bailey. If an important visitor was present, halls and chambers might be richly decorated.

Reconstruction illustration showing the arrangement and layout of the keep as built in the 12th century. The drawing shows the five main levels of the keep, from the basement to the level of the gallery above the Upper Hall, all connected by the main stair in the turret on the right

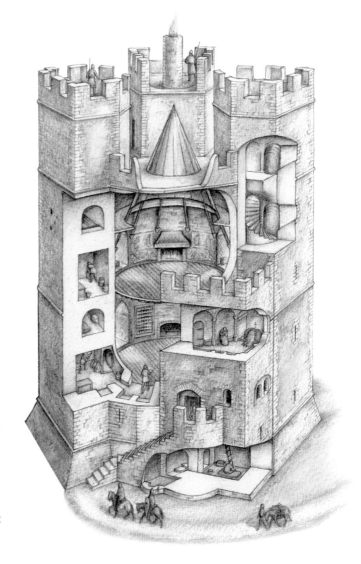

THE LOST WALLS OF ORFORD CASTLE

All that remains of the outer defences of Orford Castle is the confused area of earthworks surrounding the keep, and there have been many theories about the position of the vanished fortifications. One valuable source of evidence has been the range of historic illustrations of the castle, from the 16th to the 19th century, but they are often contradictory. What was required was firm physical evidence, and in 2002 a fresh series of archaeological investigations was commissioned in an attempt to locate the walls, or at least to provide information for a reconstruction of the early castle.

The first task was to produce an accurate survey of the earthworks. In addition, a geophysical survey was undertaken to search for traces of buried stonework. Both surveys pointed to an area north of the keep where stonework of the lost walls

and towers might survive, and a small-scale excavation here revealed a section of the curtain wall.

As a result of these investigations, our understanding of the defences

Orford Castle, town and estuary from the north.

© SKYSCAN BALLOON PHOTOGRAPHY

has grown (see pages 2-3 for reconstruction drawing). Much remains uncertain, especially south of the keep, but we can at least confirm that the walls and towers shown in John Norden's drawing of about 1600 (right) have a firm basis in reality.

The keep seems to have stood within a small bailey, enclosed by a curtain wall with (probably) six projecting towers and a gateway. An outer ditch, about 15 metres wide, lay some distance in front of the wall, perhaps suggesting an original plan to build a larger bailey. The deep ditches now visible close to the keep on the south and west almost certainly result from the demolition of the wall and the quarrying of its stone for re-use.

The entrance lay on the south-west. Stonework is still visible in the 'causeway' here and a small excavation showed that two substantial walls formerly flanked a passage leading to the entrance gate. This walled passage may have connected the gateway with a bridge across the outer ditch (the building of a stone bridge is mentioned in the Pipe Roll for 1172-3), but further excavation will be needed before we have a reliable picture of the entrance and indeed of the whole defensive plan at Orford.

Orford Castle, recorded about 1600 by John Norden, just before the loss of its outer walls and towers. The reconstruction drawing on pages 2-3 is based on Norden's view, and on the earthworks, geophysical survey and excavation evidence

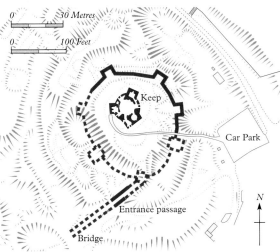

0   30 Metres

0   100 Feet

Keep

Car Park

N

Entrance passage

Bridge

Plan of the earthworks immediately around the keep, with the conjectural line of the vanished walls and towers which formerly enclosed the castle bailey

Right: The double latrine beyond the kitchen, once divided into two cubicles by a now-demolished wall

Window alcove in the Lower Hall, with the stone bench which encircles the hall and the entrance to the stair which leads up to the Constable's Chamber

The shallow stone sink with drainage hole, set in the wall of the kitchen

Many of the walls may have been plastered and painted, with the beams and roof timbers colourfully decorated, and hangings and brightly painted furniture would have been brought in.

The hall is well lit by daylight from the window alcoves, each with its pair of flat-headed windows under a round arch, and with an arched vault. Note the marks of the timber planking which supported the rubble and mortar vaults while they dried. There was no glass in the windows, but wooden shutters could be closed against the dark and the weather. Light as well as heat came also from the great fireplace, which originally had a tall stone hood on brackets before being altered later in the Middle Ages.

The window alcoves also led to rooms in the turrets and the thickness of the walls. If you want to explore all the passages on the way up, the tour goes around each floor in a clockwise direction, starting from the entrance, taking each alcove in turn, and finishing back at the main stair.

KITCHEN

Step up into the alcove next to the doorway by which you entered.

Note the heavy wear on the step from centuries of use. A passage leads to the kitchen in the west turret. The two small fireplaces and single stone sink seem inadequate for a major feast in the Lower Hall, and there was

probably a larger kitchen outside in the bailey. But it would be useful for heating food, or cooking for the smaller numbers normally resident in the castle, and it was essential if the castle was attacked and defenders were holding out in the keep.

Beyond the kitchen is a double latrine, its two seats formerly separated by a short wall. The term garderobe, given then and now to such arrangements, is equivalent to the present-day 'cloakroom'. Ammonia given off by the latrine may indeed have helped to protect any robes stored there against insect attack. Perhaps it was in order to restrict odours and increase privacy that the entrance direct from the Hall was blocked soon after building. Ventilation from the two slit windows was, however, probably fairly effective, and shows the care taken at Orford with sanitary arrangements. At each level the latrines are concentrated in this turret, their chutes disgorging together at the foot of the building.

CONSTABLE'S CHAMBER

Back in the Hall, take the next alcove and climb the spiral stair to the passage and chamber in the north turret.

The room's advantages suggest that it was for an important official, probably the constable of the castle himself. It was private, away from the public area of the Lower Hall but warmed by the chimney from the great fireplace, and its window faces east to catch the rays of the morning sun. Some of these benefits are shared by the chambers above and below, but one is unique – the urinal through the outer wall of the passage, saving a long walk down the stair and across the hall. In the passage,

notice also the neatly vaulted ceiling, shaped to accommodate the arched top of the door as it opened. The doors themselves have long gone, but you can still see such evidence for them in most of the passages, showing a concern for both security and privacy.

Back in the Hall, cross to the next alcove and turn left down the passage.

The North Chamber, warmed by the Hall fireplace, was another room of some status, perhaps a bedchamber for middle-ranking visitors to the castle. Further round the Hall is the doorway to the main stair, which fills the south turret and connects all levels of the keep from basement to roof. Like most such stairs it rises clockwise, giving a right-handed defender space to wield his sword, while hindering an attacker coming from below. As you descend to the basement, notice again the marks of the planks which supported the underside of the stair as the mortar dried. It was evidently difficult to get single slabs long enough for the full width of the stair, and the steps were made up from shorter pieces.

BASEMENT

The basement held supplies of food and water, essential at all times but especially when the castle was under siege, with recesses at the foot of the

An unusual convenience: the urinal formed through the wall of the keep in the passage just outside the Constable's Chamber

Lower left: Chambers in the turrets are approached by passages formed in the thick walls of the central tower. This is the passage to the King's Chamber on Level Four

Plan of Level One (basement)

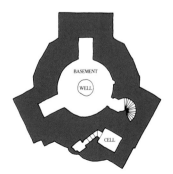

The well in the basement, with one of the two vaulted recesses for storage at the foot of the turrets

The main staircase. Notice the marks of the boards which supported the mortar below the stairs as it dried

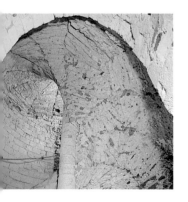

turrets for extra storage. The central well-shaft is formed from finely cut stone blocks to a depth of nearly 14 metres, a splendid example of medieval engineering. The water was possibly rather salty, but fresher supplies could be obtained by collecting rainwater into the cistern, high up in the building, which we shall see later. The basement has a stone sink, and a smoke vent in one of the recesses to allow a fire to be lit. Probably both of these were to do with the preparation of foodstuffs for storage or for consumption.

Climbing back up the stair, pass the Lower Hall and take the next passage to a set of rooms devoted to the religious life of the castle.

CHAPEL AND CHAPLAIN'S CHAMBER

First comes the chapel, which is formed in the restricted space above the lobby. This is the most richly decorated interior within the keep. Around the walls are a series of decorative arches, the deepest of which contains the remains of the stone altar table. In the wall beside the altar is a basin or piscina for washing the sacred vessels; notice that one side of this has been cut away to make it easier to use. There are also two cupboards for storing liturgical objects. Preserved on the walls are traces of the original 12th-century decoration: a skim of white plaster trimmed around the arches to create chevron patterns. Only a small group of similar plaster schemes is known, all of them in the south-east of England. To the left of the altar is a squint that allowed people to hear divine service from the passage. Just beside the chapel door is a raised board. It conceals the slot for the portcullis that closed the main entrance below.

Further along the passage is the chaplain's chamber. He needed to be close to the chapel to say the regular daily services, and will have lived in his chamber probably in no great comfort. But beyond his room he had his own latrine (the best preserved in the castle) and a store-cupboard for clothes and books.

The chapel as it appears today, and as it may have looked in use during the 12th century

Plan of Level Three

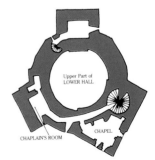

Early 20th-century visitors in the Upper Hall. The stone blocks above the fireplace helped to support the great conical timber roof which once covered the hall, as reconstructed in the drawing opposite

Opposite page: Feasting in the Upper Hall of the castle, a reconstruction illustration by Alan Sorrell

Plan of Level Four

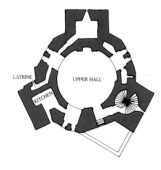

UPPER HALL

Continue up the stair, past the passage which led to the roof of the forebuilding, (originally a fighting platform for defence of the keep, now inaccessible), and into the Upper Hall.

This now appears similar to the Lower Hall, but when built it was a much more splendid space, intended with its associated chambers as an apartment for the most important visitors, including, if necessary, the king himself. The room would then be decorated with hangings and equipped with furniture, lights and precious vessels. Its splendour was enhanced by the original form of the roof – a high conical or domed construction, supported by the thirteen projecting stone corbels around the walls. Circular rooms and roofs like this are mentioned in medieval literature and descriptions of the palaces of Byzantium (modern Istanbul), capital of the Eastern Roman Empire. Its creation at Orford may reflect the breadth of learning of whoever designed the castle for King Henry, and their desire to associate the king with the great monarchs of antiquity.

The hall lost its conical roof as the castle decayed through the 17th and 18th centuries, but a similar roof was recreated in 1831, when the Marquis of Hertford carried out repairs. The present flat roof was installed in the 1930s and renewed in the 1960s, with steel beams clad in oak. The fireplace,

like that in the Lower Hall, was altered in late medieval times. It originally had a projecting stone hood, carried on the small shafts each side with their sculpted human heads, the left-hand male, the right-hand female.

The first alcove leads to an upper kitchen, for cooking or for heating food prepared elsewhere. The single, round-arched fireplace has a fireback of roof-tiles in herringbone pattern, and there is a drain at floor level. It seems probable that the room doubled as a washroom, where servants could supply noble visitors, immersed in a wooden tub, with water, heated at the fire and afterwards conveniently poured down the drain.

The windows on this side of the hall give good views of the earthworks south-west of the castle. The walls have vanished and the earthworks have been blurred by time, but the banks and ditches in this direction are still reasonably clear. Beyond them is a platform, where a beacon is shown on a map of the 1570s. John Norden, thirty years later, showed a similar beacon blazing from the top of the keep. These beacons were used in times of crisis, and acted as a guide and warning to ships out at sea.

THE KING'S CHAMBER

The next alcove leads to a chamber in the north turret, with its own latrine located conveniently across the recess

Window alcove in the Upper Hall. The glazing of the windows is modern – the original windows had only wooden shutters to keep out the wind and rain

Plan of Level Five

(and with evidence for two doors to keep odours at bay). Easily reached from the Upper Hall, this is the highest status room in the building, no doubt the sleeping chamber intended for the king or other great personage. The last alcove before the stair has a pair of large cupboards facing each other across the space. They were probably for the safekeeping of clothes or valuables, with heavy wooden doors and strong locks.

The exhibition in the Upper Hall, set up by the Orford Museum Trust, tells the story of the castle and the later Borough of Orford, with artefacts and copies of important historic maps, charters and other documents. In addition, a changing display provides information on the local environment and on life in Orford in later centuries.

Before leaving the Hall, look up at the doorway high to the left of the fireplace.

This doorway led to a chamber in the north turret not now accessible, but once reached by a gallery above the conical roof of the hall. If you climb further up the main stair, you can walk along the passage which led to this lost gallery. At the end of the passage the room lined with finely dressed stone is the cistern, collecting rainwater from the roofs and perhaps distributing it to other rooms through a system of pipes. Such a system was installed in Henry II's castle at Dover,

and there is a similar cistern at the top of the keep at Conisborough Castle in Yorkshire, built by Henry II's half-brother soon after Orford.

THE ROOF

At the top of the main stair you will see a structure which seems startlingly modern in a building otherwise little touched by time. The reinforced concrete platform was built early in the Second World War, initially as a gun platform although adapted as a radar observation post to keep watch on enemy activity along the coast. After the war it was retained, partly, no doubt, because of the difficulties of removing it, but also to serve as a reminder of the castle's revived role in defending the eastern coasts nearly 800 years after it was first built. Orford was important in the development of radar, with early ideas discussed at the Crown and Castle Hotel in the 1930s and experiments carried out on the Ness.

The stair ends at the modern flat roof, with the turrets rising still higher. The medieval conical roof would have kept below the level of the surrounding parapet (now destroyed) and thus protected from attackers' missiles. The tops of the turrets served as fighting platforms and watchtowers, and, originally reached by ladders, are not accessible to visitors. That on the left of the stair retains some of its battlements, with sockets in the sides of the upstanding

❖ THE VIEW FROM THE ROOF ❖

Looking over Orford to St Bartholomew's church tower and beyond, across Orford Ness to the North Sea and along the coast to the north

From the top of the keep, a magnificent panorama opens out. It seems natural to look first across Orford Ness to the open sea, before taking in the views up and down the coast. On a clear day you can see:

East – Orford Ness and the sea

- the river Ore, flowing behind the shingle spit to the sea 10 kilometres further south
- Orford Ness; its continuing growth spelled decline for the medieval port of Orford. The National Trust property here can be visited from Orford Quay
- the North Sea; treacherous currents and sandbanks have caused many wrecks over the centuries in the busy shipping lanes
- the lighthouse, built in 1795 and visible 25 kilometres out to sea. The castle and church were seamarks in earlier times
- the military airfield, used in both World Wars for armaments testing. Radar was developed here in the Second World War.
- the 'pagodas' built in the 1950s for atomic weapons research
- to the right, Havergate Island, now an RSPB reserve famous for its avocets

North – the coast to your left

- in the distance, the dome of Sizewell Nuclear Power Station
- Aldeburgh, where the river turns south behind Orford Ness
- on the Ness, the BBC World Service building and radio masts
- Orford church tower. The top, which collapsed in 1830, was restored in 1962-71.

South – the coast to your right

- Felixstowe, major container port, with Harwich beyond

West – inland

- forests on the sandy heathland; Staverton Thicks was a deer park in the Middle Ages
- towards Woodbridge, the Anglo-Saxon ship burials of Sutton Hoo (National Trust)

The entrance arch of the baking chamber in the north turret, with the firing chamber low down on its left

Decorative floor-tiles, re-used in making up the floor of the lower chamber

Plan of Roof Level

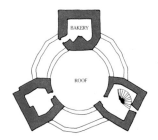

An excellent reason for climbing to the top of the keep will be readily apparent if the weather is clear – the magnificent panorama, across the estuary to Orford Ness and the open sea, and for considerable distances inland and along the coast. Details of the view are given on page 17, but the simple experience of gazing from the roof gives a very clear impression of how Orford Castle was built to command the land and shipping approaches, and how it continues to dominate its surroundings eight centuries later.

THE EARTHWORKS AROUND THE KEEP

Back at ground level, take a walk round the base of the keep. In the corner behind the northern turret is the finely built group of outfalls from the latrines. Around the keep, enclosed by the curtain wall, was the fairly restricted area of the bailey, where buildings will have stood to house the men of the garrison, stabling for horses and other necessary structures like the main kitchen.

As you look out across the earthworks, the pattern seems confused and difficult to interpret. What appears to be an inner ditch is instead the result of digging for stone and sand from the 17th century

merlons, where shutters pivoted to cover the gaps between. They were swung out to allow defenders to look or to shoot outwards, then dropped back into place.

The north turret contains the chimney from the hall fireplaces. Inside the turret is the remarkable survival of a large baking oven with a dome and entrance arch of roof-tiles, and a second firing chamber at lower level connected to it by a flue. The lower chamber has a floor made from line-impressed floor-tiles, a practical way of using up wasters spoiled in the kiln. The floor- and roof-tiles here, among the earliest examples of their kind in England, perhaps indicate the types used elsewhere in the castle when it was built, but which are now lost.

onwards, and of 19th century landscaping around the castle. However, with the aid of early illustrations and recent investigations, it is possible to suggest how the castle may have looked when first built, with a single defensive ditch (still mostly visible) set some considerable distance in front of the curtain wall and its towers (see pages 2-3, 8-9 and inside the back cover).

The finely arched outfalls from the latrines located in the western turret of the keep

❖ NATURAL HISTORY ❖

Orford Castle stands in a dramatic sweep of landscape, part of the Suffolk Coasts and Heaths Area of Outstanding Natural Beauty. On the seaward side, it overlooks salt marsh and mudflats, well known for breeding colonies of wildfowl and wading birds including redshank, lapwing and, especially on the RSPB site of Havergate Island, avocets. There are also important colonies of Black-headed and Herring gulls. Orford Ness is well known, too, for its shingle flowers – yellow-horned poppy, purple flowering sea pea, sea kale and sea campion.

Inland is a mosaic of land-use, with remnant heathland and the more recent conifer plantations

Avocet

now characteristic of the light soils of the Suffolk Sandlings. The immediate landscape setting of the castle, until recent times, was short turf grassland on the sandy soils of the earthworks, with abundant growth of gorse. This remains in places, accompanied now by scrub woodland and mature trees which

provide a range of habitats for birds and small mammals.

The turf supports a population of rabbits and, especially around the keep, of moles. The rabbits graze the turf short, encouraging grassland plants such as lady's bedstraw, sheep's sorrel and wild clary. The walls of the keep itself support a range of plants including mosses, lichens and pellitory-of-the-wall.

The former quarry to the west of the castle is of both historical and ecological value, for its scrub woodland, hart's tongue fern and, especially on the northern side, for the geological exposures of the sandy Coralline Crag stone, used in places in the building of the keep.

HISTORY OF THE CASTLE

❖

HENRY II'S NEW CASTLE 1165-73

One side of the Great Seal of Henry II, 'by the Grace of God Duke of Normandy and Aquitaine and Count of Anjou'

With Henry II's works at Orford, we can for the first time trace the whole process of building a major English castle through the accounts of money spent on it. These yearly statements of the king's income and expenditure, known as the Pipe Rolls, are preserved in the National Archive in Kew. In them we can follow the pattern of spending on the castle over the period from 1165 to 1173, with a total cost of just over £1,413. The sum seems tiny now, but was enormous by 12th-century standards, when the whole royal income for an average year was little more than £18,000. Once built at such cost, Orford remained an important royal castle for the next 150 years.

During the reign of Henry's predecessor Stephen, civil war between the king and Henry's mother the Empress Matilda led to anarchy. Barons had become used to independence and guarded against royal interference by building illegal castles. Henry was determined to bring this situation under control and to show who ruled, not just in England, but in the whole of his vast territories, from Scotland to the south of France. By inheritance, conquest and marriage he was King of England, Duke of Normandy and Aquitaine, Count of Anjou, and Lord of Brittany.

Gerald of Wales described Henry in the 1180s as having 'a reddish complexion, rather dark, and a large round head. His eyes were gray, bloodshot, and flashed in anger. He had a fiery countenance...He took little rest'.

Events gave Henry little time for relaxation. He had married Eleanor of Aquitaine in 1152 and four of their five sons survived childhood – Henry, Richard, Geoffrey and John. The whole family was to be the source of much trouble, regularly in rebellion against Henry and in alliance with his enemies, the King of France and his own belligerent barons.

Henry's first task was to reimpose authority and order throughout his kingdom. Power depended on castles, and he demanded the return of castles that had once been royal, and the destruction of those that had been built illegally. He strengthened his own major castles at Carlisle, Newcastle, Scarborough and especially Dover, and built one entirely new one, at Orford.

A major problem in East Anglia was Hugh Bigod, Earl of Norfolk (although his power base was in Suffolk) and one of the most formidable barons in England. He had four castles in Suffolk, at Framlingham, Bungay, Walton and Thetford. In 1157 Henry felt strong enough to confiscate all four. Giving Framlingham and Bungay back in 1165 in return for the payment of a heavy fine, Henry thought it would be wise to build a strategically placed castle of his own in Suffolk.

One advantage of Orford was its position between Framlingham and the coast where a foreign enemy or imported mercenaries might land. Another was the ease of supplying it with men and provisions by sea, rather than laboriously overland.

Orford is not mentioned by name in the Domesday Book account of the kingdom in 1086, and was probably included as part of the manor of Sudbourne. By the mid-12th century, however, it was already a flourishing port on the East Anglian coast, a rival to Ipswich, and it had its own market. Orford Ness, which now extends far to the south of Orford, then ended much closer to the town, providing a natural haven for shipping with easy

ILLUSTRATED BY CHARLES STOTHARD IN 'MONUMENTAL EFFIGIES OF GREAT BRITAIN', 1817

access to the sea. Perhaps Henry was also conscious of the need to maintain good communications up and down the east coast, with Orford joining Newcastle and Scarborough as strategic harbours under the protection of royal castles.

The manor was part of the honour or group of lordships based on Eye in Suffolk, which Henry had earlier given to his friend and chancellor,

Henry II, builder of Orford, and his wife, Queen Eleanor of Aquitaine. The drawing is of their tomb effigies in the abbey church at Fontevrault, on the borders of Anjou and Poitou in north-west France, part of Henry's vast continental possessions. Their son Richard I is also buried at Fontevrault

King Henry faces Archbishop Thomas Becket, in a 13th-century painted glass window in the Trinity Chapel, Canterbury Cathedral

© ANGELO HORNAK

Entry in the Pipe Roll for 1172/3, detailing expenditure on the building of 'a great ditch about the castle of Orford', together with a stone bridge and the stocking of the castle with provisions

Thomas Becket. It was taken back when Becket, appointed Archbishop of Canterbury by Henry, quarrelled bitterly with the king and in 1164 fled to France. The threat of invasion by Becket's continental friends was a further reason for Henry to want a castle on the coast, and the location at Orford was available at just the time it was needed.

The Pipe Rolls record expenditure on the new castle from 1165 onwards, but give tantalisingly little detail of the building works themselves. The usual entry is of simple amounts received or spent, confirmed by 'view' of the overseers of the accounts. The main viewers were Bartholomew de Glanville and Robert de Valoines, both important local landowners and related to the better-known Ranulf de Glanville, who would eventually become Henry's Chief Justiciar, his

principal officer of government. Bartholomew became the first constable of the royal castle. A third viewer was Wimar the Chaplain, who was made vicar of the new church being built in Orford at the same time as the castle. The king was keen to create not only a military stronghold but an expanded and flourishing market town, increasing his income from rents and dues, improving the port and draining the marshes to make good farmland for supplying his new castle with provisions.

Early items in the accounts (1163-4) cover the building of a causeway, perhaps to bring up stone from ships docked at the waterfront, and a mill to grind corn for the workmen. Work on the castle itself pressed on with considerable speed from 1165-6, when a total of £663 was spent and by the end of the next year the total had risen to almost £1,000. A major part of the castle was completed by now (almost certainly the keep) and in 1167 a payment was made 'for munition of the castle', that is, for the provision of supplies. Bartholomew de Glanville received 20 marks (£13.33), his first payment as constable.

Expenditure then continued at a lower level, presumably for work on the walls and towers: £120 in 1167-8, £134 in 1168-9. In the Pipe Roll for 1172–3 there is a final spending item 'And on building a great ditch about the castle of Orford together with a palisade and a brattice, and for

ORFORD & FRAMLINGHAM

The castles at Orford and Framlingham symbolise well the armed struggles between medieval kings and their barons. Royal Orford retains only its keep, baronial Framlingham its walls and towers, but together they show the transformation of castle defences during the period.

Orford's keep was designed to solve a problem with rectangular towers – that their corners could be undermined and brought crashing down. In theory, the projecting turrets also allowed more effective fire at attackers around the base of the keep – though they immediately created more corners again. More purposeful were the rectangular flanking towers built on Orford's curtain walls. They were also used at Dover when the great royal castle was being rebuilt a little later.

At Framlingham, demolition of Hugh Bigod's castle after his rebellion cleared the way for his son Roger to rebuild in the new style around 1190. The high walls and projecting towers of the new Framlingham, based on the model of Orford, were highly efficient in delivering fire from their parapets and arrow loops. Framlingham helps us to visualise how Orford must have looked when first built.

Where did the ideas come from? Ultimately inspired by the great fortifications of Byzantium, they do not seem to have come directly with crusaders from the Holy Land. Cylindrical towers were being built in France for some time before appearing here, and the example of Orford was not extensively copied elsewhere in England. However, the introduction at Orford of curtain walls with flanking towers was highly significant in encouraging the development of this type of fortification in the late 12th century.

Add 42130 f56 THE BRITISH LIBRARY, LONDON.UK/ BRIDGEMAN ART LIBRARY

The crossbow could be fired with greater velocity and accuracy than the long bow, though it took rather longer to prepare for firing. Border detail from the Luttrell Psalter, 14th century

Framlingham Castle from the west. Built around 1190, the walls with their projecting towers were modelled on the earlier example nearby at Orford, designed to allow flanking fire from bowmen to defend the lengths of wall in between

building a stone bridge from this same castle'. It may be that a wooden palisade was needed to strengthen the castle's defences against the risk of attack in the approaching rebellion, before the stone curtain wall was completed. The 'brattice' was a projecting wooden hoarding, built on top of a wall to allow missiles to be fired or dropped onto those attacking the wall below.

The great rebellion, 1173-4

The castle was ready only just in time. In 1173 serious revolt broke out, led by the king's son and heir, the young Henry, and involving both England and the continental possessions. In Suffolk the resentful Earl Bigod, now 80 years old, joined the revolt and landed Flemish mercenaries in Suffolk. Orford was reinforced with men and provisions: bacon, cheese and salt, along with coal, iron, tallow, ropes and hand-mills for grinding corn (though most of the coal was captured by the Flemings). Over £159 was spent in wages to the knights and sergeants of the garrison, possibly amounting to about 70 men. There was also compensation paid to a certain Ralph le Breton 'for his houses which were carried into the castle', perhaps to help accommodate the extra troops quartered there.

The rebel army landed near Walton Castle (Felixstowe) but failed to capture it. Earl Hugh decided not to attack the new castle at Orford, and also failed to operate effectively elsewhere. The Earl of Leicester, leader of the rebellion in England, was defeated near Bury St Edmunds and Henry himself defeated Louis of France on the borders of Normandy. In 1174 Bigod submitted to the king, again gave up his castles and was obliged to see them all, including Framlingham, demolished.

The man sent to direct the demolitions was Alnoth 'Ingeniator' (engineer), overseer of the king's buildings and for thirty years Keeper of the Palace of Westminster. Alnoth has been proposed as the likely designer and builder of the castle at Orford, and possibly also of the new church. This may well be; certainly, whoever planned the castle was a highly skilled and experienced designer who served Henry well. Orford was successful in strengthening the king's hold on an important part of his kingdom, although in general the rebellions did not stop. After the young Henry's death, Queen Eleanor and her remaining sons Richard and John continued to plot right up to the time of the old king's death in 1189.

Orford in the time of Henry's sons

Henry II spent more than half his reign out of England in his continental lands, and there is no

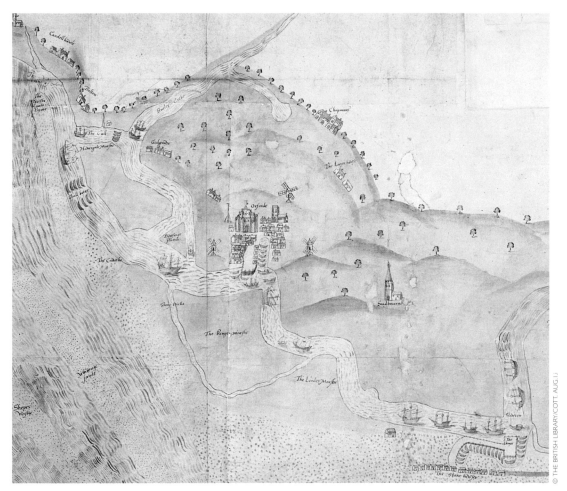

evidence that he ever saw his new castle at Orford. His son and successor Richard passed even less time in England, most of his reign being spent on crusade to the Holy Land, in captivity on his way home, or fighting in France. The king was only released from captivity on payment of a huge ransom, collected by his mother Queen Eleanor. In 1194 she assembled at Orford a fleet of ships and an accompanying military expedition to carry the money to Richard's keepers in Germany.

Orford was again a centre for military operations late in the reign of Richard's brother John, now engaged in his own struggle against rebellious barons. After signing Magna Carta in

Plan of Orford and its surroundings, including the Ness, from a chart of the Suffolk coast made in the 1570s or 80s. The castle and houses of the town are clearly shown, with shipping moored in the harbour or under sail on the river

1215, he entrusted Orford to his Justiciar, Hubert de Burgh, and sent orders to hand it over to the forces of Savaric de Mauléon, fighting for the king in East Anglia. Next year John himself was in Suffolk, capturing Framlingham Castle (by now rebuilt as we see it today) from its builder Roger Bigod, son of the rebellious Hugh. King John died in 1217, and his enemies' fortunes revived. Orford Castle was captured by the troops of Prince Louis of France, leader of the rebel lords and claimant to the English throne, along with the castles at Cambridge, Colchester and Castle Hedingham. Damage to the castle at Orford, however, seems to have been slight, and with the triumph of forces fighting for the new young king Henry III, only modest sums were needed to repair its defences.

The baronial wars and Edward I

In the Barons' War against Henry III in the 1260s, Orford Castle, still a major stronghold in East Anglia, changed hands regularly. It was twice held by a later Bigod Earl of Norfolk; when the king won it back he entrusted it to his son the Lord Edward. On 11 April 1277 Edward, now king, visited the castle. It is the only recorded occasion when a reigning monarch came to Orford in a time of relative peace, and it must have been a busy and splendid event, though conditions could still be

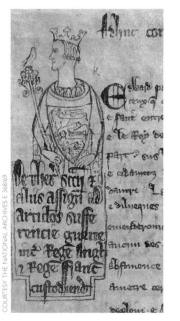

Edward I is the only reigning monarch known to have visited the royal castle of Orford, in April 1277

difficult and lawless. While the disreputable Hugh of Dennington was constable in the 1270s, he imprisoned a royal official for three days (presumably in the basement prison), and one man imprisoned by him in the castle was so badly treated that he died of his wounds, and the body was dumped at sea.

Twice more the castle was garrisoned when rebellion threatened, by Edward I in 1297 and by Edward II in 1307-8. In 1301 threepence a day (just over one new penny) was paid to '10 men guarding the castle with cross-bows, bows, arrows and other arms'. There were repairs in the 1270s, when the turrets were given new lead roofs, and in 1317-18, when over £55 was spent in repairs to the well, and to the houses, walls and other parts of the castle.

By this time, however, the castle was beginning to be leased out, marking a decline in royal interest – to Robert of Ufford (the elder) in 1280, to Roger Bigod, Earl of Norfolk in 1302, to Robert of Ufford (the younger) in 1330. Finally in 1336 Edward III effectively sold it to the younger Ufford, created Earl of Suffolk the next year. It remained in private hands from then on, no longer fulfilling its old functions as royal stronghold and centre of local administration. The estuary was silting up and the port was declining, although the town was still of sufficient importance to be made a borough in 1579.

TOWN, CHURCH, PORT & BOROUGH

Whether or not an earlier settlement existed at Orford, by 1138 there was already a successful port and a market. With encouragement from the building of the castle in the 1160s there was a chance to develop both town and port and increase royal income from dues and rents. A regular street plan was laid out around a new market place, a new church was built, and the harbour improved.

It is still possible to explore the streets of the medieval town, walking from the castle through the market place to the church of St Bartholomew, with its grand Norman chancel now in ruins. Turning down Quay Street, the Town Marsh carpark marks the site of the medieval dock, from where

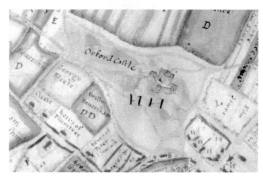

John Norden's plan of Orford about 1600, with the town's streets and houses to the south-east of the castle, and the fields and closes on the north and west

© ORFORD MUSEUM

Suffolk wool was exported to Europe. Orford was important and populous enough in the 13th century to attract the building of a friary and two hospitals.

But trade was affected by the relentless growth of the Ness and the silting of the river. Records from the 15th century reveal the life of the town, surviving on fishing,

shipbuilding, textile manufacture and minor coastal trade. Orford became a borough in 1579 with a mayor and burgesses, recorder and justices of the peace, and despite its decline continued to send two members to serve in Parliament. The borough (though not the MPs) survived the Reform Act of 1832, but was swept away in 1886, the corporation replaced by a parish council and Town Trust, which still owns the ancient records and regalia of the borough.

'Orford was once a good town, but is decay'd. The sea daily throws up more land to it, as if it was resolved to disown the place, and that it should be a sea port no longer'
Daniel Defoe 1724-6

The ruined Norman chancel of St Bartholomew's church

The castle in decline

Through the 15th and 16th centuries the castle descended, with the manor of Sudbourne, through the families of Willoughby of Eresby and the de la Pole Dukes of Suffolk. Though it began the period as an inhabited residence it probably fell gradually into disuse and decay. The keep retained some value as a coastal signalling station and landmark for ships out to sea, and the prison chamber was occasionally used to hold malefactors from the town. In the 1590s Sir Michael Stanhope bought the castle and manor from the Willoughbys. Sir Michael was born about 1552 (his father was beheaded that year), served in the Elizabethan

❖ THE LEGEND OF THE MERMAN ❖

Ralph of Coggeshall, writing about 1207, relates how:

'*In the time of King Henry, when Bartholomew de Glanville was custodian of the castle, it happened that the fishermen, fishing in the sea, caught in their nets a wild man, whom in their wonder they brought to the Castellan. He was naked and was like a man in all his members. He was covered with hair and had a long and shaggy beard. The Knight kept him in custody many days and nights, lest he should return to the sea…. Whether he would or could not, he would not talk, although oft times hung up by his feet and harshly tortured. Brought into church he showed no signs of reverence or belief…. He sought his bed at sunset and always remained there until sunrise.*'

The capture of the Merman, a woodcut by James Dodds, 1995

After such harsh treatment – perhaps in the prison chamber of the castle – the Merman eventually managed to escape back to the sea. Ralph seems uncertain about the truth of the story:

'*Whether this was a mortal man or some fish pretending to have human form, it is not easy to conclude, especially as so many tales are told about so many incidents of this sort.*'

Such traditions were indeed common round the coasts of Britain from medieval times and earlier – from Scotland to the Isle of Man, Northumberland, Kent and Devon. Mermen and similar figures of wild men are shown in medieval sculpture, including the 'woodwose' on the font at Orford. The legend of the Merman continues to be celebrated, in poetry, novels, art and drama.

Another type of medieval wild man, carved into the pedestal of the font in Orford Church

fleet and became Groom of the Chamber to Elizabeth and to James I.

It was Stanhope who in 1600-2 commissioned John Norden to draw up the survey of his new manor which so valuably illustrates the castle, on the eve of a period when its walls and towers were to be progressively demolished for their stone. Already by 1605-6 loads of stone were being taken from the castle site to make foundations for Stanhope's new buildings at Sudbourne Hall.

Norden's plans also record in considerable detail the town and surrounding landscape in a time of change – a town which had declined from its earlier importance and survived now as a minor port for coastal trade.

Sudbourne and Orford passed in 1621 to Stanhope's daughter Jane and eventually to his granddaughter Elizabeth, who in 1657 married Leicester Devereux, Viscount Hereford, a leading parliamentarian

in the Civil War. In a county which saw little fighting in the wars, the castle had escaped the fate of others elsewhere in England, of bombardment, capture and destruction. Instead, Orford slid into a period of benign neglect, during which the roofs and floors of the keep may have collapsed if they had not already done so, but when nevertheless much of the remarkable detail of the early keep survived intact.

18TH- AND 19TH-CENTURY ANTIQUARIES

The 18th-century enthusiasm for topography and antiquities brought artists and antiquaries to the site, their drawings providing important information on the remains of the castle. Samuel and Nathaniel Buck included Orford in their magisterial series of published *Prospects of English Towns and Ancient Buildings*, dedicating their view of 1736 to Price Devereux, 9th Viscount Hereford.

View of the keep and a surviving fragment of curtain wall, by S and N Buck, engraved in 1736. Also shown is the tower of Orford church and a ruined gable end of the town's medieval friary

The tomb of Sir Michael Stanhope in Sudbourne church

Orford, *engraving after a watercolour of about 1826 by J M W Turner for* Picturesque Views in England and Wales, *(1825-38)*

Charles Hartshorne remarked on the castle's generally good state of preservation, though the last fragment of curtain wall fell in 1841. The keep was furnished and occasionally used for banquets and private parties, the grounds becoming a popular place for picnics. Following the death of the 4th Marquis in 1870, his natural son Sir Richard Wallace inherited much of his father's vast fortune, as well as his interest in collecting art and historical material. In 1871 Wallace also bought Sudbourne Hall with Orford Castle from the 5th Marquis. He sold it in 1885 (to Sir Arthur Heywood), and died in 1890, but items relating to Orford were included in the superb Wallace Collection, bequeathed to the nation by his widow in 1897 and established in Hertford House, London.

In 1753 Orford and Sudbourne were sold to the Earl of Hertford. His heir the 2nd Marquis proposed in 1805 to pull the castle down, but was persuaded by the government to retain it as a valuable seamark for ships attempting to navigate the dangerous sandbanks off the coast. In addition, during the Napoleonic wars (1793-1815), the castle's ancient role of defence against a foreign invader was revived. A wooden stair was built to provide access to the semi-ruinous building and in about 1812 a signalling mast was erected on the south turret, as part of a coastal network.

Antiquarian interest in the castle encouraged changing attitudes to the preservation of medieval remains. In 1831 a new floor and conical roof were provided by the 3rd Marquis, though the chapel remained ruinous, without roof or floor. In 1840 the Rev

Sir Richard Wallace, a portrait commissioned by the people of Sudbourne from the local artist W R Symonds to mark Wallace's sale of the estate in 1885

ORFORD IN THE 20TH CENTURY

A series of sales from 1918 marked the end of the Sudbourne estate's connection with the castle and it failed to meet its reserve at a sale in 1928. The castle was bought, and presented to the Town Trust in 1930 by Sir Arthur Churchman. A new roof and floors were made (of steel and concrete covered with oak), and items of local historical interest were displayed in the Upper Hall, as they had been earlier.

During the Second World War the castle was requisitioned and the radar observation post built on the top of the south turret. Some damage was done during the war years, and items from the collections in the keep inevitably went missing (although many have since been recovered by the Orford Museum Trust). There were also some destructive, though on the whole small-scale, alterations made inside the keep; the dividing wall in the first-floor latrine was removed at this time. At the end of the War, the desire to erase the 'vandalism' of the concrete platform on the south turret was resisted, in order to preserve evidence for this 20th-century revival of the castle's ancient role in coastal defence.

In 1962 the castle was transferred by the Town Trust into the Guardianship of the Ministry of Works, and has remained in the care of its successors, the Department of the Environment and, from 1984, English Heritage. The Orford Museum Trust has undertaken responsibility for the town's collections and history, and has mounted the exhibition on the history of the castle and town in the Upper Hall.

The historic connections between Orford Castle and Sudbourne are now commemorated by the two cannon displayed on modern carriages by the carpark. These two 6-pounder naval guns of about 1800 are said to have come here from Sudbourne Hall, having perhaps been originally brought ashore to play their part in local defence against the threat of Napoleonic invasion.

View of the castle from the south-east in 1785, an engraving by S Hooper. All that then survived of the castle was the keep and one small fragment of curtain wall, which finally collapsed in 1841

Looking across the earthworks, south-west from the keep. The ditch in the foreground marks the position of the lost wall, with the medieval defensive ditch beyond

The castle today

Attention now concentrates on developing a better understanding of the castle and its wider history, through research into the extensive documentation for castle and town, building studies of the well-preserved keep, and surveys of the earthworks, above and below ground. These are undertaken by English Heritage partly to answer questions about historical aspects of the site, and make for improved interpretation and services for visitors. But they also allow better-informed protection and conservation of the site. A building as ancient as Orford Castle, subject to hostile marine weather conditions, needs constant maintenance and regular repair if it is to survive in good condition into the future. The aim is a sustainable balance, where the fabric of the building is made safe while its essential character is preserved, so that future generations too may have the enjoyment and understanding of a unique building.

Further Reading

Jane Allen, Valerie Potter and Margaret Poulter, *The Building of Orford Castle; a translation from the Pipe Rolls*, 1163-78, Orford Museum, 2002.

R. Allen Brown, *Orford Castle, Suffolk*, London: Department of the Environment/HMSO, 1964.
English Castles (revised edn), London: Chancellor Press, 1970.

H.M. Colvin (ed), *History of the King's Works: The Middle Ages*, London: HMSO, 1963.

Paul Drury, 'Twelfth-century floor and roof tiles at Orford Castle', *Proceedings of the Suffolk Institute of Archaeology*, 36 (I), 1985.

T.A. Heslop, 'Orford Castle, nostalgia and sophisticated living', *Architectural History (Journal of the Society of Architectural Historians)* **34**, 1991.

Tom McNeill, *Castles*, London: Batsford/English Heritage, 1992.

Derek Renn, *Framlingham and Orford Castles*, London: English Heritage, 1992.
Norman Castles in Britain, London: John Baker, 1968.